SHE
HE
THEY
THEM

UNDERSTANDING GENDER IDENTITY

by Rebecca Stanborough

Consultant:
Melissa Trevathan-Minnis, Professor of Psychology
and Counseling, Goddard College

COMPASS POINT BOOKS
a capstone imprint

Informed! is published by Compass Point Books, an imprint of Capstone.
1710 Roe Crest Drive
North Mankato, Minnesota 56003
www.capstonepub.com

Library of Congress Cataloging-in-Publication Data is available on the Library of Congress
website.
ISBN: 978-0-7565-6413-1 (library binding)
ISBN: 978-0-7565-6561-9 (paperback)
ISBN: 978-0-7565-6414-8 (ebook PDF)

Summary: She/he/they/them. Why do we use gender pronouns? And why do some people wish
to be referred to as "they"? What is gender identity all about? Students will learn to understand
these terms and the reasons behind them. They will also learn how to deal with questions they
may have about gender identity.

Image Credits
Alamy: gameover, 31; Associated Press: The Free Lance-Star/Peter Cihelka, 5, Office of the
Speaker of the House Nancy Pelosi/Julio Obscura, 48; Getty Images: Transcendental Graphics,
40; Michelle Bisson: 30 (top); Newscom: Sipa USA/Alex Milan Tracy, 22, SOPA Images/Graham
Glendinning, 16, ZUMA Press/Brian Cahn, 56, ZUMA Press/Robin Rayne, 25; North Wind
Picture Archives: 20, 30 (bottom); Shutterstock: Africa Studio, 38, Antonio Guillem, 41, DFree,
32, Double Brain, 13, 14, Gluiki, 19, J. Bicking, 51, Justin Starr Photography, 8, Monkey Business
Images, 46, rblfmr, 6, VectorMine, 11, Soleil Nordic, 15; SuperStock: Underwood Photo Archives,
21 .
Design Elements: Shutterstock

Editorial Credits
Editor: Michelle Bisson; Designer: Brann Garvey; Media Researcher: Eric Gohl; Production
Specialist: Kathy McColley

Consultant Credits
Melissa Trevathan-Minnis, Professor of Psychology and Counseling, Goddard College
Sensitivity reader: Sabra L. Katz-Wise, PhD (she/her), Assistant Professor, Department of
Pediatrics, Harvard Medical School; Research Associate, Division of Adolescent/Young Adult
Medicine, Boston Children's Hospital

Author's Note
I am a white, middle-class, cisgender writer. Though I aimed for accuracy and compassion, I may
have made mistakes in what I've decided to include and leave out, and how I've written about this
important subject. I own those mistakes and apologize for them wholeheartedly.

All internet sites appearing in back matter were available and accurate when this book was sent
to press.

Printed and bound in the USA.
PA99

TABLE OF CONTENTS

CHAPTER ONE

A Gender **Revolution**—and Reaction

It was a hard lockdown.

Students huddled in secured locker rooms, practicing how to keep safe if an active shooter entered the school. Boys huddled in the boys' locker room. Girls huddled in the girls' locker room.

One student was left to face a wall in the hallway, completely alone.

The teachers in the Stafford County, Virginia, middle school didn't know which locker room the student should use. The student was transgender. And because the school district had no clear guidelines about where she belonged, that student was sent into the hallway by herself.

"If there was someone armed," she told a local newspaper, "I would've been the first one gone."

The separation of a transgender student from other students during an active shooter drill led a large group of supporters to attend a school board meeting to protest the school's actions.

This event was a drill, not an actual active shooting. But the fact remains: a transgender student was left in a hallway on her own because the school district had not made it clear that her right to safety was as important as every other student's.

Across the nation, conflicts over the civil rights of transgender people are taking place in businesses, schools, hospitals, and government agencies.

Newspapers are full of headlines like these:

"Transgender HS Student Says He Was Removed from Prom King Ballot"
Atlanta Journal and Constitution, March 21, 2019

"Administration Moves to Revoke Transgender Health Protection"
The Washington Post, May 24, 2019

"Supreme Court to Rule on Gay, Transgender Employment Rights"
Wall Street Journal, April 22, 2019

Yet, even as transgender rights are being challenged in courts and classrooms, some parts of U.S. society seem to be making strides toward accepting gender differences. Some people are fighting for progress on these rights, while others are pushing back.

People understand more now ever before about the science of sex and gender. Social media have created new ways for people of different genders to express themselves. Customers are questioning product categories like "girl toys" and "boy toys." And athletes are breaking gender barriers in lots of different sports.

Customers may be questioning boy and girl toy separation, but girl-focused aisles full of dainty dolls and boy-focused aisles teeming with trucks are still commonplace.

For some people, that feels like good news. For others, it may feel like the world is changing too fast.

Even language is changing. The gender revolution has given rise to a new vocabulary. *Transgender, cisgender, gender-fluid, genderqueer, nonbinary, ze,* and *zir*—these words represent different ways of describing ourselves and each other.

Gender Lexicon

Here's a quick look at some of the terms that are making news:

- **Cisgender:** a person whose gender identity matches the sex they were assigned at birth.
- **Gender-fluid:** a person whose gender identity changes at different times.
- **Genderqueer:** a person whose gender identity is not limited by society's gender norms.
- **Gender nonconforming:** a person whose gender expression—such as clothing and behavior—doesn't follow society's norms.
- **Nonbinary:** a person whose gender identity is neither strictly male nor female, as our society defines those genders.
- **Transgender:** a person whose gender identity does not match the sex they were assigned at birth.

Are these words just a social trend? Or might society finally be acknowledging identities that have been part of the human experience all along?

People in the U.S. are hotly debating what should be done about the needs of people who don't fit into tidy gender boxes. Many government policies—like the Virginia school district's—do not protect the rights of transgender people. And that means people are being left out and put in danger.

All over the United States—and in many places worldwide—people have gone on the march in support of equal rights for gay and transgender people.

Why does it arouse such strong feelings when someone assigned one gender at birth feels that they belong to another gender? Or that they don't relate to any one gender? That's what will be explored in this book, along with cultural conflicts that have arisen with the recent expansion of our understanding of gender identity.

CHAPTER TWO

What Is **Gender Identity?**

Gender identity is the sense of one's own gender. For some people, naming their gender is relatively easy; they see themselves as men or women, boys or girls. But those two categories don't work for everyone. Some people see themselves as somewhere in between. Or both. Or neither.

It's important to point out that gender is a core part of overall identity, but it isn't the only part. Other parts of identity—like race, culture, sexual orientation, faith, social class, and family connections—might be just as important to a person's sense of self.

Because of the way our society is organized, gender identity and gender expression have a powerful influence on people's lives. Gender can determine a person's friends, toys and games, fields of study, and even the jobs and professions that they choose. It can even influence how much money people are likely to make as adults.

The Roots of Gender Identity

In *How to Understand Your Gender*, authors Alex Iantaffi and Meg-John Barker say that gender is "bio-psycho-social." That is, your gender is influenced by your biology, your psychology, and your society.

Your understanding of your gender is shaped partly by your biology. It may be influenced by your body parts and the chromosomes and hormones inside you. You have an innate understanding of who you are. That understanding may or may not line up with how other people see you. It may or may not line up with the body you see when you look in the mirror.

Your gender is also influenced by your social surroundings. Your family, friends, school, church, neighbors, people on social media—even strangers—all have a lot to say about how you should act based on how they see your gender. These social rules and opinions may or may not make sense to you.

For the most part, gender identity stays the same over a lifetime. But it is possible that as your body, mind, and culture change, how you see your gender might also change over time.

Let's look first at the "bio" part of the "bio-psycho-social" gender equation.

Hormones

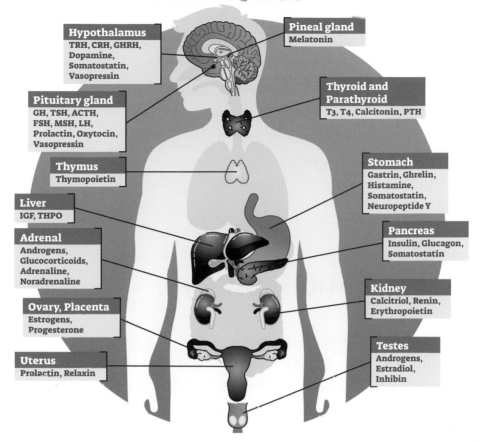

Hypothalamus
TRH, CRH, GHRH,
Dopamine,
Somatostatin,
Vasopressin

Pineal gland
Melatonin

Pituitary gland
GH, TSH, ACTH,
FSH, MSH, LH,
Prolactin, Oxytocin,
Vasopressin

**Thyroid and
Parathyroid**
T3, T4, Calcitonin, PTH

Thymus
Thymopoietin

Stomach
Gastrin, Ghrelin,
Histamine,
Somatostatin,
Neuropeptide Y

Liver
IGF, THPO

Adrenal
Androgens,
Glucocorticoids,
Adrenaline,
Noradrenaline

Pancreas
Insulin, Glucagon,
Somatostatin

Kidney
Calcitriol, Renin,
Erythropoietin

Ovary, Placenta
Estrogens,
Progesterone

Testes
Androgens,
Estradiol,
Inhibin

Uterus
Prolactin, Relaxin

Sex Assigned at Birth

When a baby is born—sometimes even before a baby is born—a medical professional assigns a sex—male or female—to the baby. That assignment is usually made based on the baby's external genitals. It may also be made based on chromosomes or hormones. This sex assignment is a legal label. It shows up on birth certificates, school records, and all sorts of other official documents. Most of the time, the sex assigned at birth lines up with the gender that develops. But not always.

Checking in

This book is a basic primer on the subject of gender. If you've never given much thought to these issues, or if you've given a LOT of thought to them, you might discover that the subject makes you a little (or a LOT) anxious. Take breaks if you need some time to process what you're reading. Breathe slowly, drink water, take a walk—and come back when you're ready.

Bodies and Biology

For a long time, U.S. society has looked at assigned sex and gender as the same thing. Doctors, nurses, and parents look at a baby's body and say, "It's a boy!" or "It's a girl!" But external genitals aren't a foolproof method of deciding a person's sex.

For one thing, external genitals (such as a vulva or penis) and internal genitals (such as ovaries) don't always match. And sometimes a person's genitals aren't that easy to categorize because they don't look clearly female or male, as our society defines male and female bodies.

Another biological factor that has been used to assign sex is chromosomes. Your body is made up of approximately 37 trillion cells. Each cell contains tiny threads called chromosomes. Your chromosomes carry a kind of genetic map that tells your body how to develop.

Almost everyone has 46 chromosomes in their cells (23 chromosomes from one parent and 23 from the other). Usually, people with 46 XX chromosomes develop bodies that look female. And most of the time, people with 46 XY chromosomes develop bodies that look male. But not always. Sometimes people have extra X or Y chromosomes, and those can change the way sexual characteristics, such as genitalia, develop.

And then there are hormones.

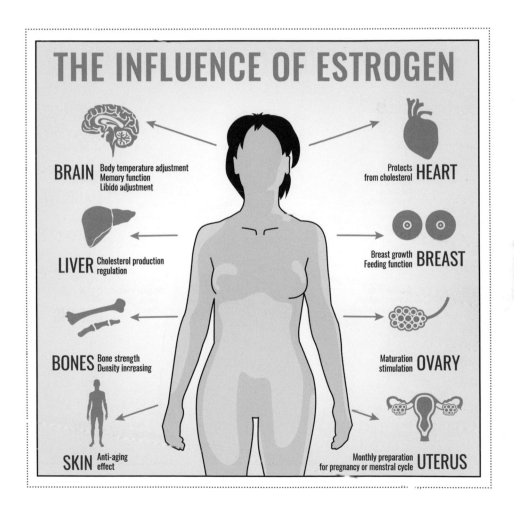

Hormones are chemicals in the body that play a large role in sexual development. Testosterone and estrogen are two of the major hormones. Everyone has both testosterone and estrogen working inside them. These chemicals determine whether a person develops characteristics that look male or characteristics that look female. But not everyone processes hormones the same way. So hormone levels aren't always an accurate way of assigning sex either.

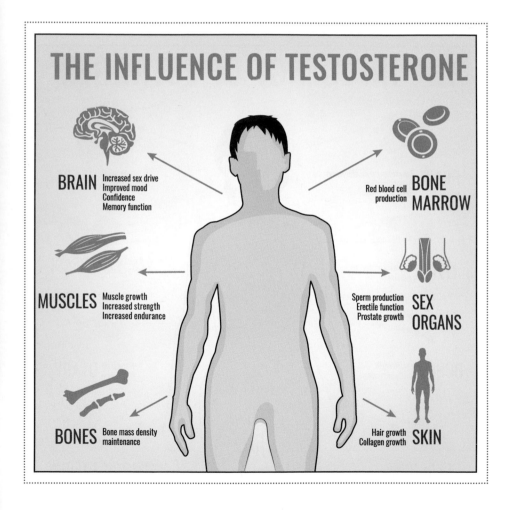

THE INFLUENCE OF TESTOSTERONE

BRAIN Increased sex drive
Improved mood
Confidence
Memory function

Red blood cell production BONE MARROW

MUSCLES Muscle growth
Increased strength
Increased endurance

Sperm production
Erectile function
Prostate growth SEX ORGANS

BONES Bone mass density maintenance

Hair growth
Collagen growth SKIN

Intersex People

Just like gender identity, sex is not limited to two strict categories.

About 2 percent of the world's population have genitals, hormone levels, or chromosome patterns that aren't typical. Maybe they have really high testosterone levels. Maybe they have extra X or Y chromosomes. Or their genitals may be hard to assign to either a female or male category. The umbrella term used to describe all of these natural differences is *intersex*.

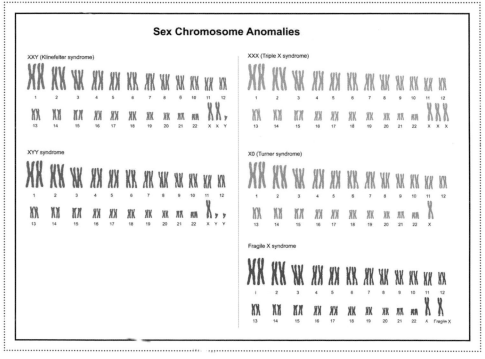

Most people have 23 pairs of chromosomes for a total of 46, but sometimes, babies are born with fewer or more than that number of chromosomes.

Caster Semenya Outruns Her Critics

Her face shone with sweat and triumph. It was May 2019 and Caster Semenya had just won her 30th 800-meter race. But if the International Association of Athletics Federations (IAAF) had its way, it would have been her last.

The IAAF adopted regulations that would require Semenya to take drugs to lower her testosterone if she wants to keep racing as a woman.

Semenya's body naturally produces high levels of testosterone. In adopting the regulations, the IAAF said that the hormone gave her an unfair advantage over other female runners. Semenya, in protest, brought this case to the Court of Arbitration for Sport (CAS), the highest court in sports.

In a 2-to-1 decision in May 2019, CAS ruled that "the regulations adopted by [the IAAF] are discriminatory but necessary to ensure fair competition" among female athletes.

Joanna Harper is a transgender athlete and medical adviser to the International Olympic Committee. Harper said, "High testosterone is the most important factor that separates male and female athletes."

But not all medical experts agree that testosterone is so important. Sometimes athletes with lower testosterone beat runners with higher levels. And other physical traits could create just as much of an athletic advantage. Olympic swimmer Michael Phelps's body produces half as much lactic acid as most other people's bodies. Some say this gives him extra endurance in the water. Yet Phelps is not asked to take drugs to change his body chemistry.

Some people think that Semenya is being targeted because she is black or because she defies other gender norms. Millions of Semenya's fans love her exactly as she is. What matters to them is watching her run. She says she's not stopping any time soon.

"I'm going to keep on doing what I do best, which is running," she says. "I want to inspire the world. I want to show them nothing is impossible."

Semenya appealed to a Swiss supreme federal court. In July 2019, the court temporarily upheld the ban but Semenya continued to appeal.

For a long time, doctors believed that they should pick which sex an intersex child would be. After the doctors chose, they would do surgery to change the child's body to match the doctor's idea of the baby's sex.

The children were too young to understand or agree. Parents and doctors often kept the kids in the dark about what had been done to them. And sometimes the doctors chose the wrong sex. That choice created a lifetime of confusion and pain for the intersex child.

Many doctors now believe it is better to wait for an intersex child to get older so they can have a say in the process. The World Health Organization says doctors should not operate on intersex children unless there is a medical reason to do so. The risks to the physical and emotional health of the child are too great.

The medical profession has come a long way, but some doctors still do surgery on intersex children when they are very young.

Bodies are incredibly diverse. And while physical bodies sometimes line up with gender identity, the two don't always agree. And that is 100 percent okay.

CHAPTER THREE

The **Gender Binary** and Beyond

In the U.S., gender has historically been limited to two categories: male and female. Hospitals mark either female or male on birth certificates. When parents register children for school, camp, or sports teams, the same two options are available.

Because we have traditionally seen people as one or the other of these two categories, our gender system is binary. The prefix *bi* means "two." That means there are usually two choices for bathrooms: women's and men's. Two boxes to check on all official forms. Two soccer teams: one for boys and one for girls. Plus men's and women's jails, homeless shelters, and dressing rooms.

Having a strictly binary gender system is a problem for two big reasons. One, gender really isn't binary. Plenty of people don't fit into either one of those two tidy boxes.

The other reason the gender binary system is a problem is that those two categories of people get treated very differently. Men historically have had more political, social, and economic power than people assigned to the female category. Rigid definitions of what it means to be male and female keep that power imbalance in place.

It isn't healthy or fair for half the population to be held back by the other half just because of gender. And it isn't healthy or fair if people who don't fit neatly into either box are penalized because of their gender. And it also isn't fair if someone other than you gets to decide to which category you belong.

If gender isn't truly binary, then society is making life really hard on nonbinary people (those who don't identify as girls/women or boys/men) for no good reason at all.

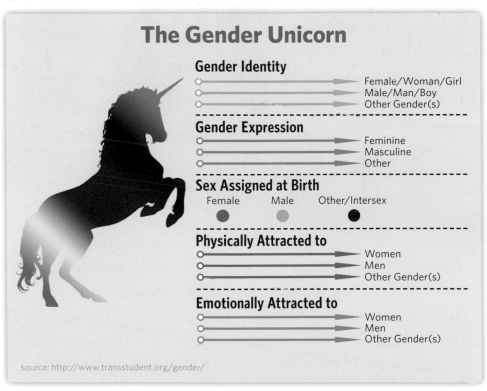

The Gender Unicorn is used to explain the difference between gender identity, gender expression, assigned sex, and sexuality. The arrows show that people can be anywhere on a spectrum in each of these areas.

Beyond the Binary

There is plenty of historical evidence that it has never been accurate to lump all people into either female or male categories.

Take a look at the life of Thomas/Thomasine Hall. Historical records from the 1620s show that Thomas or Thomasine lived as both a woman and man at different times and places. Assigned female at birth, Thomasine cut off her long hair at 22 years of age and enlisted in the army as a man.

After the war, Thomas went back to living as Thomasine. She moved to Plymouth, England, dressed as a

Like many women at that time, Thomasine Hall used her talent for sewing to make a living.

woman, and earned a living sewing lace. Some time later, Thomasine immigrated to the Virginia colony in America and appeared in society sometimes as a man and other times as a woman. Some residents objected and brought the case to court. The court ordered Thomas/Thomasine to wear both pants and a woman's cap to indicate a blended gender.

Another example is the New York politician Murray Hall. Assigned female and named Mary Anderson at birth in 1804, Hall left Scotland for the United States wearing the clothing of his brother, who had passed away. He lived the rest of his life as a man. He married, adopted a child, and was elected to public office at a time when women could not even vote. In an effort to keep his female body parts a secret, Hall did not get medical help when he needed it and later died of breast cancer. It's worth noting that the thing that made the other politicians mad was not that he had kept this secret from them. They were mad because he had voted.

After he settled in the United States, Murray Hall became a politician with Tammany Hall, the organization that controlled New York City politics for about a century.

These two people defied the gender traditions of their day. They lived beyond the binary at a time when strict rules governed what it meant to be a man or a woman.

It's impossible to know how many people have lived beyond the binary in U.S. history but it's certain that these are only two of many such stories.

Transgender People

People who are transgender (or trans) have a gender identity that differs from the sex they were assigned at birth. (The prefix *trans* means "beyond" or "across.")

Some transgender people know at a young age that their gender identity does not match what other people expect of them. Some people become aware later, when they are teens or adults.

Some children know that they are transgender and are willing to fight for their rights.

Many trans people experience feelings of anger, confusion, and anxiety. Those feelings are perfectly logical given the amount of pressure there is to live up to other people's gender expectations. Negative feelings can be even more intense for trans people who are teased, bullied, or hurt because of their gender identity.

Different Ways of Transitioning

Many transgender people—but not all—take steps to move from living as one gender to living as another one. People transition in different ways.

Some people transition socially. They may wear different clothes at home or in public. They may also change their hairstyles to better match their gender identities. They may ask people to call them different names or refer to them with different pronouns. They may change their name legally or have a ceremony with people who support them.

Some people may make physical changes to their bodies by taking hormones or having surgery. It's important to know that not everyone wants to take these steps.

It's also important to understand that not everyone has access to the medical care they need to make physical changes. In the U.S., there is a shortage of doctors who know how to care for transgender people. And then there's the cost: transitioning can be expensive. Some people cannot afford the care they need. Some insurance plans don't cover the cost of transitioning.

The Amsterdam Method

Starting around 2007 at a gender clinic in Amsterdam, doctors pioneered a three-stage transition process for young transgender people. It was called 12-16-18. At around 12 years of age, young people could take hormones that blocked puberty. The purpose of taking these hormones was to prevent the development of secondary sex characteristics, traits that make a person look more female (e.g., breasts) or male (e.g., facial hair or a lower voice). The effects of these drugs were reversible.

At around 16 years old, patients began taking drugs called cross-sex hormones or gender-affirming hormones to start medical transition. These hormones made permanent changes to the body. At age 18, when people could legally consent to surgery, surgeons altered the body so that it matched the person's gender identity. For example, surgeons might have removed the breasts of someone who identified as a boy/man. Or they might have changed genitalia from a penis to a vulva and vagina if a person identified as a girl/woman.

A 2014 study tracked a group of 55 transgender youth as they transitioned with the 12-16-18 approach. At the age of about 21, and at least one year beyond gender reassignment surgery, a large majority of participants were satisfied with the results and functioning happily.

The Amsterdam program has been available for some time in the U.S. The number of gender clinics is growing. Some of these clinics use a similar approach to the Amsterdam program. Other gender providers and clinics take a more flexible approach. These providers consider when an individual person is ready to move to the next stage, rather than starting at a certain age. But not every trans person can afford this care if they need it. And not every trans person wants surgery.

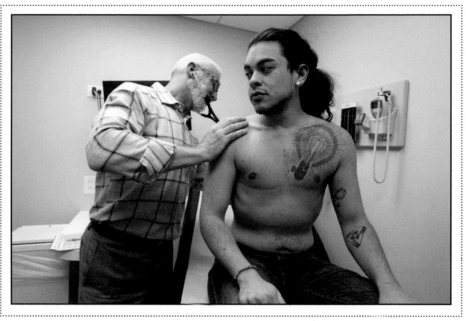

Clinics in many parts of the U.S. treat transgender patients such as TK Hadman, age 30, who said he struggled with gender until he transitioned to male six years ago. "I'm totally at peace in my true gender," he said.

How, when, and where transitions take place are personal matters.

Trans people deserve respect. Unless you are a close personal friend, don't ask people to share the details of their transitions with you. Even if you are a close friend or family member, let people decide how much they want to share with you about their journeys.

Fact

A pronoun is a word that replaces a noun. Look at this sentence: "When Geri is playing soccer, she's a beast!" The word *she* is a substitute for the noun *Geri*.

Cisgender

The word *cisgender* refers to people whose gender identity mostly aligns with the sex they were assigned at birth. Being cisgender means that you aren't trans.

Cisgender Privilege

If you are cisgender, you were born with privileges that trans people don't enjoy. For example, you might not have to worry much about your gender identity. When you are cisgender and need to use a bathroom, you can easily choose which one to use. People probably don't ask you about your body parts. People don't question your name or call you pronouns that make you feel uncomfortable. You probably won't be stared at because of your gender identity. You needn't worry about losing your job or your loved ones if someone finds out about the sex you were assigned at birth or your gender identity. And you probably won't have to fear being made fun of, insulted, hurt, or killed because of your gender identity.

Many find it heartbreaking that people must live in fear because of how others respond to their gender identity. But that is today's reality.

Fact

Cis-sexism is discrimination against trans people because of their gender identity.

Nonbinary Identities

Some people do not identify as either a girl/woman or a boy/man as U.S. culture defines them. The term *nonbinary* is an umbrella term for people who identify with aspects of both genders, or who don't identify with either binary gender. People might refer to themselves as *genderqueer*, *neutrois* (gender-neutral), *agender* (having no gender), or *pangender* (identifying with all genders), or by another identity label. If people experience their gender as changing from time to time, they may refer to themselves as *gender-fluid*. Some nonbinary people identify as transgender, but others do not.

It's important to listen to people about which gender identity labels feel right for them. Though it may look like someone has a particular gender identity, the only way to know for sure is if that person tells you.

Sexuality

You may be wondering what your gender identity has to do with your sexuality or sexual orientation. Who you are romantically or physically attracted to is separate from who you are as a person. Some people who identify as boys/men are attracted to other boys/men. Some people are attracted to girls/women. Some people are attracted to nonbinary people. Some people are attracted to more than one gender. Some people are not attracted to anyone at all. Sexuality and the identity labels people use to define it are as complex as gender identity.

CHAPTER FOUR

Bustles and Bowties: What Is **Gender Expression?**

Transgender icon Janet Mock remembers the day the school dress code caught up with her. She'd been wearing dresses to school for a while. Even though other students insulted her, she kept wearing what made her feel good. Then one day the vice principal stopped her.

"You're making people uncomfortable," she remembers him saying. Wear a dress again, he told her, and they'd send her home. She wore a dress again. And he sent her home. Again and again. Finally, with her mother's support, Janet transferred to a new school.

Janet Mock, like millions of other transgender people, found a way to express her true self in a world that wanted to limit her.

Gender Expression

Gender expression is how you present your gender to the world around you. Gender identity is inside you. Gender expression is something the outside world can see. Your gender expression might include the way you dress and wear your hair. It might include the way you walk, sit, or speak in public. It might also include your name and the pronouns you use to refer to yourself.

Gender expression doesn't have to match your internal gender identity or what others expect based on your assigned sex. How you express your gender can vary from day to day, depending on where you are, who you are with, how you feel, and what you are doing. Other people may notice how you express your gender. They may comment on it. Their comments may be uplifting or hurtful. In some situations, you may have to change your gender expression to keep yourself safe. Ultimately, you are the best judge of how to present yourself to the world around you.

Toys Are Us

Gender pressure starts early. Think about the toys you played with when you were younger. Were they pink? Blue? Did you notice more cars in "boy" toy aisles in the store? More dolls and cooking toys in "girl" aisles? The people who create and sell toys are guiding girls toward some activities and boys toward others. Even toys that all kids play with, like LEGO blocks, have pink and lavender versions for "girls."

Studies show that kids know which toys they are supposed to like, depending on their gender. Researchers also know that when no one is looking, kids sometimes branch out and play with other toys that are not meant to be for their gender.

Bustles and Bowties

Society has a lot to say about how gender should be expressed. For a very long time, clothing reflected the idea that gender is binary. Women and men were expected to dress differently. From colonial times until the 1970s, women were expected to wear skirts and dresses. Until World War I and beyond, those dresses went all the way to the floor. Layers of petticoats were heavy and hot and kept many women from being physically active. They went out of fashion around the 1890s.

For centuries, women had to wear floor-length dresses no matter what kind of work they did.

Women have also been expected to wear uncomfortable undergarments. For decades, middle- and upper-class women had to wear corsets. Corsets fit around the waist. They were pulled tight to create an hourglass body shape. In the early 1900s, corsets went out of fashion because they kept women from being able to move freely. They could also damage internal organs.

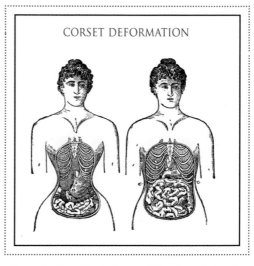

CORSET DEFORMATION

Corsets literally deformed the female body.

In the late 1800s, women also wore bustles. They fit around the waist, adding a pouf to the back of a woman's dress. Like corsets, bustles kept women from moving naturally.

For a long time, suits and pants were considered appropriate only for men. In fact, if a woman made the decisions in the home, people said she "wore the pants in the family." Ties, belts, and suspenders were also considered part of a male-only wardrobe. As more women entered the workforce in the 1900s, they began wearing suits and pants too.

Today, women's and men's clothes are much more similar. But even though the clothes people wear are now often androgynous, some schools still have dress codes that treat girls and boys differently. In most clothing stores, clothes are still separated into girls' and boys' sections.

It is still taboo for boys to wear dresses, skirts, and other clothes that are seen as feminine. And in certain settings—prom, for example—it is still unusual for girls to wear clothing that is seen as masculine, like a tuxedo. Mostly, girls who dress in traditionally masculine ways are not treated

Billy Porter rocked the 2019 Oscar *Vanity Fair* after-party with his beautiful black dress and full beard.

as badly as boys who dress in traditionally feminine ways. Billy Porter, the Emmy, Grammy, and Tony award-winning star of the show *Pose*, says it this way: "We've moved beyond the idea that women wearing pants is a problem. . . . Women wearing pants is powerful and it's strong, and everybody accepts it. It's associated with being male. The minute a man puts on a dress, it's disgusting. So what are we saying? Men are strong. Women are disgusting. I'm not doing that anymore."

Dressed to Express

For many transgender and gender-nonconforming people, shopping for clothes is a tricky business. But in recent years, gender-neutral, norm-defying clothing lines have sprung up everywhere. From bespoke New York City tailors Bindle & Keep (the subject of the HBO documentary *Suited!*)

to gender-expansive kid clothiers like Girls Will Be, Free to Be Kids, Cat & Jack, and Boy Wonder, people can dress to express more than ever before.

Paying Attention to Pronouns

In the English language, most pronouns reflect a binary understanding of gender. We say *he*, *she*, *him*, and *her*. For lots of people, these gendered pronouns don't work.

There are many reasons why a person might feel uncomfortable with a certain pronoun. The main reason is probably that it doesn't fit their gender identity. Even though it is natural to be curious about why someone has decided to change pronouns, it's probably not a good idea to ask why. If they want to tell you, they will.

Sometimes a pronoun that is usually used for another gender feels better to someone (e.g., a person who was assigned female who now identifies as a boy and uses *he/him* pronouns). Sometimes neither *he* nor *she* feels quite right to someone.

Enter nonbinary pronouns. Some people want to be referred to as *they* or *them* because these pronouns don't have genders associated with them. But others don't want to be use those terms. They have created a whole range of alternate gender-neutral pronouns—words like *ze* (pronounced zee) and *hir* (pronounced here).

It takes courage to ask other people to use a different pronoun than the one they are used to using. If you're not sure what a person's pronouns are, you can ask.

It is really important to ask about pronouns privately. If you ask a person in front of others, you could be outing someone in a place where they are not safe.

When you introduce yourself to someone new, you can let them know which pronouns you use. An introduction that includes your pronouns opens the door for your new acquaintance to share their pronouns with you.

Pronouns are small words, but they have a big impact on how people see themselves and others. Respecting someone's pronouns shows your respect for the person.

Gender Pronouns

Please note that these are not the only pronouns. There are an infinite number of pronouns as new ones emerge in our language.

Subjective	Objective	Possessive	Reflexive	Example
She	Her	Hers	Herself	She is speaking. I listened to her. The backpack is hers.
He	Him	His	Himself	He is speaking. I listened to him. The backpack is his.
They	Them	Theirs	Themself	They is speaking. I listened to them. The backpack is theirs.
Ze	Hir/Zir	Hirs/Zirs	Hirself/ Zirself	Ze is speaking. I listened to hir. The backpack is zirs.

Source: http://www.transstudent.org/pronouns101/

Here are just a few of the pronoun options available. It may take a little time to get used to using the ones that are not familiar to you.

Misgendering People

If someone you know has changed their name or pronouns, you may sometimes make a mistake and use the old ones that you are used to using. If you accidentally use the wrong name or pronouns, just apologize, correct your mistake, and move right along.

Avoid making a huge apologetic fuss, so that the other person doesn't feel pressure to take care of you and your feelings. A better way might be to practice the right pronouns later, so you don't keep making the same mistake.

In *The Trans Allyship Workbook*, Davey Shlasko recommends that you practice using pronouns on inaminate objects. You can assign a pronoun to, say, a desk, use it out loud for a couple of days, and then change the pronoun and practice again. If you train yourself to pay attention to pronouns and practice them often, you'll be communicating respect to the trans people in your life.

Deadnaming

It is one thing to call someone by their former pronouns out of habit, and then correct yourself. But it is deeply disrespectful not to use a person's chosen name if you do so on purpose—and do so repeatedly. When people refer to a trans person by their former name—their birth name or the name they had before they transitioned—it is called *deadnaming*. But using the right name can have a profoundly positive effect. A 2018 study found fewer symptoms of depression among trans youth who could use their chosen name at home, school, work, and with friends. As with pronouns, you can practice using someone's chosen name when you are not with them so that you don't make the same mistake the next time you see them.

Misgendering, misusing pronouns, and deadnaming people are examples of microaggressions. Microaggressions are subtle words or acts that leave people feeling erased, insulted, afraid, or discriminated against.

If you've always been part of the social or racial majority (for example, cisgender and/or white), it's easy to think of microaggressions as small mistakes. But if you've ever experienced sexism, cis-sexism, or racism, you know that microaggressions only look small. In reality, they can pile up. They can drag down your self-esteem and eat away at you for a long time.

CHAPTER FIVE

Gender Roles
and Norms: How Society Shapes Us

In Canberra, Australia, the uncle of a baby-to-be slams his foot down on the gas pedal. His car tires squeal as he whips around in "donuts" in the parking lot. Out of the tailpipe, plumes of blue smoke make the big announcement. It's a boy!

The "burnout" this uncle performed is part of the wildly popular "gender reveal" party trend. Parents announce whether they're going to have a boy or girl through elaborate stunts.

Gender reveal parties keep alive the idea that babies are born into one or another specific gender.

Those blue billows are a hint of things to come. Society makes a big deal of a person's gender. How you see your gender is heavily influenced by the time and place where you were born. Your lived experience—how it feels to be the gender you are—is also shaped by your culture.

Culture is a system of values and norms. Your culture is created by the people who live where you live. This includes your family, your friends, your teachers, your church leaders, your government, and even your ancestors. As you grow up, you are taught about what genders exist. You're taught how you should act, speak, feel, dress, and plan for your future—all based on your gender.

Gender Norms

Norms are written and unwritten rules that show people how to act within society. Some norms involve forms of address. For example, in some parts of the southern U.S., children are taught to say "Yes, ma'am" and "Yes, sir" (notice the gendered language) when speaking to adults.

There are also norms for how to ride on buses, elevators, and subways. It's considered rude to leave your backpack on a seat when there isn't room for everyone to sit down. When people ride in elevators, they normally face the front. The norm in U.S. culture is to try to leave as much personal space as possible between one another.

There are also norms involving clothing for different occasions. For example, many people in the U.S. wear black to funerals, but in China and Mexico, people often wear white when they have lost a loved one.

Lots of norms are gendered. In cultures all over the globe, expectations for girls and boys differ. Studies show that many cultures expect girls to pay close attention to how they look. They are also expected to be polite and obedient.

Boys, on the other hand, are taught to be brave and strong. Being brave and strong are good qualities. But sometimes, the culture sends boys the message that they have to hold in their emotions. They must be "tough." Too much of that message could keep boys from being able to express their real feelings or make healthy friendships. Some studies have explored what happens when boys express only anger. Researchers found that those boys had a higher risk for drug use and behavior problems at school.

Our culture also has some unhealthy gender expectations for girls. One such message has to do with vulnerability. Boys are allowed increasing freedom as they become teenagers. But teenage girls are protected by their parents because girls are often seen as vulnerable. Too much of that message can teach girls to be passive—to wait for things to happen instead of taking risks and making decisions.

Toni Stone and her male teammates often practiced together before games.

Toni Stone

In 1953, when the United States was deep in the era of racial segregation, Toni Stone made it to the big leagues. At 32 years old, she was the first woman to play baseball in the Negro Baseball League. And was she good! One year, her batting average was .364—fourth in the league. Toni Stone played second base, called up to take home-run champ Hank Aaron's place on the Indianapolis Clowns team. From there, she went to Kansas City to play for the Monarchs.

Toni Stone started out with two strikes against her. One, she was a black woman born in the Jim Crow era. Two, she was a woman who wanted to play baseball. She experienced double discrimination. But those who knew her said she was strong and single-minded. In a 1991 interview, Toni Stone said her parents disapproved.

"It was kind of a disgrace, but I didn't care," she said. "I wanted to play baseball."

Gender Roles

Gender roles are the behaviors, attitudes, and actions we associate with maleness or femaleness. The word *roles* hints that gender roles may be something we perform for others.

Today in the U.S., boys are still expected to be protective, powerful, and aggressive. Girls are expected to be caring and empathetic. The trouble is that these ideas are based on stereotypes. They don't take into account individual differences. And they rob people of the opportunity to express themselves in ways that feel authentic.

Some gender expectations involve emotions. When boys cry, for example, they are often told that crying is for girls. Girls and women are told they are not supposed to get angry. In reality, anyone can feel sad, wherever they fall on the gender spectrum. And there are sometimes really good reasons for people to get mad.

In U.S. culture, boys are still supposed to be tough, not sad, and girls are supposed to be sweet, not mad. Those models are hard on real people, who have a range of emotions.

The Reaction to Nonconformity

Research shows that people put pressure on one another to conform to gender expectations. Parents are the most powerful influencers when it comes to gender norms. Peers are a close second. People who don't conform to gender expectations are often bullied or discriminated against.

Studies also show that boys who don't conform to gender norms are treated worse than girls who don't. A boy who wears makeup to school is likely to be teased and bullied a lot more than a girl who plays a tough sport.

Why do some people react so strongly when others defy gender norms? Researchers have begun studying that question. So far, they have found that people:
- may feel that their own gender identity is threatened by someone who doesn't fit into the accepted categories.
- may believe that the natural order of the world will be turned upside down by expanding gender beyond the binary.
- worry that their safe spaces will be invaded by people who don't belong.

Fear seems to be at the heart of the resistance to gender-nonconforming behaviors.

The Role of Religion

Our faith traditions are powerful gender shapers. This may be because certain gender expectations are enshrined in teachings that are considered holy and unchangeable. These teachings are an important part of our cultural heritage, but they may not reflect the ideals of a democratic society where everyone's civil rights matter.

For example, some faith traditions teach that women must submit to men. Many faiths also teach that certain roles should be carried out by one gender or the other. For example, child-rearing is sometimes considered the role of women only. Leadership positions are often reserved for men only. In the same way, some religious teachings make men and women the only acceptable gender identities.

When people are taught that being gender nonconforming is against God's will, it makes it easier for people to justify violence. After all, if God can send trans people to hell, aren't people being godly if they, too, harm trans people? These examples may seem extreme, but they could be influencing some of the violence against trans people.

Other Cultures, Other Genders

Cultures vary from place to place. Some cultures have more than two genders. In the book *Transgender History in the United States*, researcher Genny Beemyn talks about American Indian nations in which at least four gender identities exist.

Beemyn says, "Within most of these cultures, male- and female-assigned individuals who assumed different genders were not considered to be women or men; rather, they constituted separate genders that combined female and male elements."

The term *Two-Spirit* refers to a third gender in American Indian communities. Because this term belongs to these cultures, it's important not to take it and use it if we do not belong to those cultures.

Many American Indian societies recognize more than two genders in people. The term *Two-Spirit* is an umbrella term used to talk about these identities.

Third Genders Around the Globe

Not all cultures see gender as binary. Here are a few international examples of gender categories that exist between women and men, or represent a combination of the two genders.

Fa'afafine

In the South Pacific island of Samoa, fa'afafine are assigned male at birth. Sometime during childhood, they begin dressing and identifying as women. Fa'afafine also perform traditionally female ceremonial dances, and they do female caregiving work in their villages. Fa'afafine have been part of Samoan culture for centuries.

Hijras

In India and Bangladesh, hijras are a third gender. Assigned male at birth, hijras identify as women. Though they were once considered almost sacred—bringing blessings at weddings and births—they were treated as outcasts during the British colonial era. Some of that discrimination still happens today. However, in 2014, India granted them special status as a third gender, so hijras now have access to government jobs and education.

Mahu

Before Christian missionaries arrived on the islands of Hawaii, a third gender existed: male bodies in possession of "female sweetness." Called Mahu, this third gender allowed male and female characteristics to be blended in one body. Mahu held roles as healers and teachers, but they were not accepted by Western missionaries. Today, after generations of colonization, transgender people are subject to high levels of violence in Hawaii.

Muxe

In several regions of Mexico, a third gender exists. Muxe are assigned male at birth, but they often identify and express their gender as women. Traditionally, they have been an important part of the local economy, which thrives on fiestas. More recently, Muxe are beginning to work in other jobs, but they sometimes have to dress as men in order to do so.

Bacha Posh

In Afghanistan, having a son is considered a blessing. Sons can earn money and carry on the family name. Daughters, on the other hand, are sometimes seen as a burden. Some families have found a way around the perceived shame of having no male kids. They reassign a daughter's gender in early childhood. This practice is called *bacha posh*.

A bacha posh daughter dresses like a boy. She has freedoms ordinary girls do not share. She can play sports. She can get a job. She can shop on her own. But there can be problems for bacha posh daughters when they reach puberty because they can no longer hide their gender. Sometimes they don't want to live as girls. They may even be harassed or harmed on the streets. Many of them end up feeling caught between genders in a very strict society. Read more about bacha posh daughters in *The Underground Girls of Kabul* by Jenny Nordberg.

The Right to Resist

Some of the most interesting people are those who defy norms and live creatively. However, there is often a price to be paid for bucking tradition.

Your safety should always be a top priority. After that, it is up to you to decide which norms matter. You may decide to follow certain older traditions because they allow you to be part of a community you love. You may decide to abandon a norm or change a role that no longer works for you.

Society puts a lot of pressure on tweens and teens to conform to stereotypes, but it's most important to learn what you really feel and to be who you are.

Whatever you decide, it is not okay for someone to taunt, torment, or hurt you because you do not conform to society's gender expectations. If you are targeted, reach out to someone you trust.

CHAPTER SIX

Gender Equity:
There's Work to Do

When President Donald Trump stepped up to the podium to give his 2019 State of the Union address, a small cadre of decorated military service members were in the audience. These special guests were invited by members of Congress. They were there as a reminder of the estimated 10,790 transgender people serving in the military either on active duty or in the reserves.

But their service to the nation may be cut short by their commander in chief. In 2017, the president proposed a ban on all transgender people serving in the military. In January 2019, the U.S. Supreme Court cleared the path for the ban to continue.

U.S. Navy Petty Officer Megan Winters, a transgender woman, said, "The news of the transgender military ban, and the realization I may not be able to serve my country, felt like a core aspect of my identity was being ripped apart. My military career is as important and sacred to me as my own gender identity, and for the first time, my future is uncertain."

Before the 2019 State of the Union address, House Speaker Nancy Pelosi (left) gave commemorative coins to Major Ian Brown (right) and other members of the military in thanks for their service. Major Brown, who was awarded two Bronze Stars, transitioned from female to male during his time in the military.

The ban was based partly on the cost of providing care for transgender service members, which may include gender-affirming medical care such as hormones and surgeries. But those costs are said to be around $8 million, which is roughly 1 percent of the military's health budget.

The ban on trans people in the military is one of several recent challenges to the rights of transgender citizens in the U.S. These challenges highlight the need for gender equity. Gender equity means that all people are treated fairly, regardless of their gender identity or gender expression.

Health Care

Just like everyone else, trans people need good health care. Being transgender is not a medical problem. It is not a mental health issue. It's just one of the many differences that exist among people.

Nevertheless, it can be hard to find doctors who are willing to treat transgender people—even for conditions that aren't related to their gender identity. And those doctors who are willing to treat a transgender person are not all trained in the unique needs of transgender patients.

Under federal law, it is not legal for doctors or insurance companies to discriminate against trans people. But it can and does happen anyway. A 2015 survey found that 55 percent of trans people had been denied transition care or hormone therapy.

Even when services are covered, transgender people sometimes have to wait for a long time or travel long distances to get ordinary medical care. When they arrive, they are sometimes treated by staff who do not understand the needs of transgender people. For example, a health care worker might refuse to use pronouns that are different from the ones in a patient's medical records. They might refuse to treat the patient. Transgender people have even been made fun of in emergency rooms in the U.S.

When trans people have to worry about how medical staff will treat them, they may avoid going to doctors or hospitals. This could mean they don't get care when they need it.

In some places, health care for trans people is getting better. At the University of Louisville School of Medicine, medical students learn all about the needs of trans and gender-nonconforming people. The program is called the eQuality Project. New York's Mount Sinai Hospital opened a new Center for Transgender Medicine and Surgery. Students there can specialize in transgender care.

But these changes are not happening everywhere. And there has been pushback against these changes in some parts of the government.

In 2018, the Department of Health and Human Services launched a Conscience and Religious Freedom Division. That division has published a rule that allows health care facilities and health care workers to refuse to provide certain services that conflict with their religious beliefs. The language of that rule doesn't refer to gender identity, but some advocates worry that the rule could allow people to refuse to provide medical treatment to trans people.

Bathrooms, Locker Rooms, and Dressing Rooms

The bathroom debate has gotten a LOT of media attention. Some schools allow transgender and gender-nonconforming students to choose which bathroom to use. Other schools have built all-gender bathrooms where trans kids can feel safe. But there are still schools that say students must use bathrooms and locker rooms that match the sex they were assigned at birth.

In 2017, 16 states tried to pass laws to force people to use the bathroom that matched the sex they were assigned at birth. Only one state, North Carolina, succeeded in actually passing a bathroom bill. When the state lost millions of dollars in business as a result, it repealed the bill.

In 2018, the U.S. Department of Education said that it would not investigate reports from transgender students who are not allowed to use the right bathroom at school. Some people think that decision could put the health and safety of transgender kids at risk. Transgender kids now have to rely on their individual school districts to meet their needs—and school districts don't always do that.

Many who lived in North Carolina protested the passage of what was called the HB2 bill. After its passage, when many businesses boycotted the state, it lost so much revenue the legislature repealed the law.

Bathrooms can be dangerous places for transgender people. One recent study showed that trans kids who can't use the right bathroom are sexually assaulted at a higher rate than others. To avoid the problem, some transgender kids won't use school bathrooms—which can lead to infections and other health problems.

Trans activist (and *Supergirl* TV show star) Nicole Maines was one of the first to fight in court for equal access to school bathrooms. When her school assigned her to a gender-neutral bathroom for adults, she thought it would be okay. But eventually, she said, "It came to sort of just end up feeling lonely. It made me feel like I was an Other."

SAFE SCHOOLS LAW

States that have laws protecting LGBTQ students in schools, including bathroom laws

No law protecting LGBTQ students

Law prohibits bullying on the basis of sexual orientation only

School regulation or teacher code prohibits bullying on the basis of sexual orientation and gender identity

Law prohibits bullying on the basis of sexual orientation and gender identity

Law prohibits bullying on the basis of association with someone with a listed characteristic

Source: http://www.lgbtmap.org/
equality-maps/safe_school_laws

Fair Housing

Transgender people also face discrimination when it comes to safe housing. To find safe housing, people need to have money. But sometimes, employers and coworkers discriminate against trans people at work. That can make it hard for transgender people to keep their jobs. Without steady jobs, there may not be enough money to pay for rent in safe areas.

Even if money is not an issue, sometimes landlords discriminate against transgender people. One study involving 2,000 properties found that landlords don't toll transgender renters about all of the available properties. Other studies have found that landlords sometimes quote higher rents to transgender people.

The National Center for Transgender Equality says 35 percent of transgender people have experienced discrimination when they've try to find somewhere to live. Nationally, one in five transgender people has been homeless at some point.

The problem of anti-trans discrimination is worse for homeless people. The U.S. Department of Housing and Urban Development is planning a new rule. It would allow homeless shelters to ask about a person's gender identity when deciding whether to offer that person shelter. This means transgender people may face discrimination in homeless shelters.

Self-Harm and Suicide Risk

Some transgender people—but not all—may experience something called gender dysphoria for a period of time. Gender dysphoria is anxiety, anger, and sadness that comes from a disconnecton between the person's assigned gender and the gender with which they identify. Sometimes gender dysphoria can be severe.

Some trans people may also experience minority stress. Minority stress is the anxiety that can come from being part of a group that is treated unfairly. Trans and gender-nonconforming people are sometimes criticized, questioned, and attacked. They may be treated badly by people they know. They may be treated badly by strangers in real life or online, or both. And that kind of stress takes a toll on health after a while.

Sometimes the lack of acceptance is so bad that trans people try to hurt themselves or take their own lives. A three-year study by the American Academy of Pediatrics found that more than 50 percent of male transgender students and just under 30 percent of female transgender students between the ages of 11 and 19 had attempted suicide. Among nonbinary teenagers, 42 percent had tried to kill themselves.

Recognizing the risks for trans people is a solid first step to changing these statistics. Learning how to support, befriend, and fight for trans people is a necessary next step.

Checking in

Learning about discrimination, risk, and violence can leave you feeling shocked, sad, and angry. You might find it helpful to write about, talk about, or draw your response to what you've read. Have you ever witnessed a trans person being treated disrespectfully? Have you ever participated in making fun of a person who defied our culture's gender norms? What can you learn from your experiences? Have you ever been the target of people who treated you badly because of your gender identity or expression? If you need to take a break from reading, please take good care of yourself. It may help to talk to a supportive peer or adult about your feelings.

Violence

Transgender people in some communities are at high risk of violence. In recent years, violence against trans people has risen.

Murders of Transgender People by Identity

- Trans Woman 87%
- Trans Man 4%
- Other Trans Identity 9%

Murders of Transgender Women by Race

- Black 80%
- Latinx 10%
- Native American 5%
- White 5%

Source: https://www.glaad.org/

These pie charts illustrate who is most at risk of violence. They make it clear that danger is highest for black trans women, who are living at the intersection of three oppressed groups (black, female, and transgender).

Each year on November 20, people gather to mark the Transgender Day of Remembrance, when community members honor those who were violently killed because of their gender identity or expression. In 2018, these trans women and trans men were memorialized:

Christa Leigh Steele-
  Knudslien
Cathalina Christina James
Viccky Gutierrez
Keisha Wells
Celine Walker
Sasha Garden
Tonya Harvey
Vontashia Bell
Zakaria Fry
Dejanay Stanton
Phylicia Mitchell
Shantee Tucker
Amia Tyrae Berryman

Londonn Moore
Sasha Wall
Nikki Enriquez
Karla Patricia Flores-Pavon
Ciara Minaj Carter Frazier
Nino Fortson
Regina Denise Brown
Gigi Pierce
Tydi Dansbury
Roxana Hernandez
Keanna Mattel
Antash'a English
Jesse Sumlar
Diamond Stephens

The Transgender Day of Remembrance is marked by candlelight vigils around the world. In Palm Springs, California, members of the community gathered in 2017 to honor the memory of those killed because of their transgender identity.

Gender violence is a major reason why people immigrate to other countries. Amnesty International reports that trans women are targeted in high numbers. Among the recent transgender immigrants to the U.S. from Central America, 88 percent had suffered gender violence.

The Rainbow Railroad

In more than 70 countries, it is illegal to be gay, lesbian, bisexual, or transgender. In seven of these countries, being transgender means a death sentence. The Rainbow Railroad helps gay and transgender people escape countries where their lives are in danger because of their gender identity or sexuality. Since 2006, this organization has helped more than 600 people get to countries where they can live in freedom. The U.S. is no longer one of the most popular destinations. Today, the Netherlands, Canada, and Spain are where most gender-nonconforming people want to go.

The bad news is that gender-based violence against transgender people is still a crisis worldwide.

The good news is that awareness of the problem is growing.

Thousands of gender warriors and activists in every country are addressing gender equity. The United Nations, Amnesty International, and many governments and aid organizations across the globe are working to improve the lives of gender-nonconforming people. Big changes are underway to give transgender people equal access to jobs, health care, and safe living conditions.

Gender identity—and the freedom to express it—is in the headlines everywhere we look. For every advance, there seems to be resistance. Some of the opposition to a gender revolution is quiet. Some is violent.

Our gender landscape is gradually changing. Whether those changes will be for the good may be up to a new, gender-courageous generation.

GET INVOLVED

Many of the challenges facing transgender people are hurdles that have to be overcome at the national level. Laws need to be changed. Court cases need to be won. Financial resources need to be channeled to people who need them.

But you can also do a LOT to make life easier, safer, and friendlier for trans people where you live.

Social justice educator Dr. Barbara Love says there are four ways to stand up for the rights of people whose rights are threatened:

1. Be aware. Keep your eyes open. You may see trans or gender-nonconforming people being mistreated or excluded. You might start noticing other problems, such as forms with just two gender options, or places where bathrooms could be an issue.

2. Analyze what you notice. Think about why things are the way they are. Think about how things could change to make people feel safe and accepted.

3. Act. It's probably not enough just to say to a trans friend, "I support you." Use the right names and pronouns. If you can do so safely, interrupt when others are doing or saying hurtful things.

4. Be accountable. Listen to your trans friends about how you could support them better.

And, you can also take these steps:

Find out what your school's bathroom policy is. If you think the policy is unfair to trans kids, write a letter to your school principal and your school board members. You could also write a letter to your local newspaper explaining the problem with bathrooms in your school.

Be a bathroom buddy. If you have a friend or family member who is trans or gender nonconforming, let them know that you are available to go into the bathroom with them if it makes them feel safer.

Talk to teachers about class routines that are unnecessarily gendered. If your teacher groups students according to gender, you could gently explain to that teacher how uncomfortable those situations can be for some students. It might be a good opportunity to suggest a lesson on gender-neutral pronouns!

March!

When there are rallies, marches, protests, vigils, or days of remembrance in your area, go. Just show up, even if you're not personally connected to the organizers. Your presence will be seen and felt.

Interrupt!

If you observe someone using inappropriate language to describe or address a trans person—even if they're just using pronouns incorrectly—take a moment to educate that person about the harm they could be doing.

A word of caution: Be thoughtful about involving school authorities or law enforcement unless you feel someone is in danger. Sometimes when we involve authorities, it can backfire for the trans person. The best way to find out whether involving authorities is a good idea is to talk to your trans friend about it first.

GLOSSARY

advocate—a person who supports a cause

androgynous—appearing gender-neutral

authentic—being what someone seems to be; genuine

bespoke—made to fit a particular person

binary—having two parts

chromosome—a strand of proteins that carries genetic information

culture—a group of people's beliefs, customs, and way of life

discriminate—to treat certain people unfairly, usually because of their race, religion, age, sexual orientation, or gender

hormones—substances that regulate body processes, such as growth and sexual development

stereotypes—a fixed idea that many people have about a thing or a group that may often be untrue or only partly true

taboo—an act that is discouraged or forbidden within a culture

Critical Thinking Questions

1. Were you ever taught that certain behaviors, jobs, or activities were more for one gender than another? How would you rewrite those gender rules if you could?

2. Can you think of a toy that is unnecessarily gendered? Explain what it is and why you think so.

3. Think about the characters in your favorite TV show or movie. Is your favorite show upholding or defying gender stereotypes? Explain why you think it is or is not doing so.

ADDITIONAL RESOURCES

Further Reading

Gonzales, Maya Christina. *The Gender Wheel: A Story about Bodies and Gender for Every Body*. San Francisco: Reflection Press, 2018.

Iantaffi, Alex, and Meg-John Barker. *How to Understand Your Gender: A Practical Guide for Exploring Who You Are*. London: Jessica Kingsley Publishers, 2017.

Jennings, Jazz. *Being Jazz: My Life as a Transgender Teen*. Toronto, Ontario, Canada: Ember, 2017.

Shlasko, Davey. *Trans Allyship Workbook: Building Skills to Support Trans People In Our Lives*. Guilford, VT: Think Again Training, 2017.

Stevenson, Robin. *Pride: Celebrating Diversity & Community*. Guilford, VT: Think Again Training, 2017.

Internet Sites

Explore resources for LGBTQ students
https://www.aclu.org/library-lgbt-youth-schools-resources-and-links#transgender

Know Your Rights: A Guide for Trans and Gender Nonconforming Students
https://www.aclu.org/other/know-your-rights-guide-trans-and-gender-nonconforming-students?redirect=know-your-rights-guide-trans-and-gender-nonconforming-students

National Center for Transgender Equality
https://transequality.org/

Trans Lifeline
https://www.translifeline.org/

Trans Student Education Resources
http://www.transstudent.org/

SOURCE NOTES

p. 5, "If there was someone armed…" Jeff Branscome, "Stafford Superintendent Apologizes to Transgender Student Amid National outcry," *The Free Lance-Star*, October 9, 2018, https://www.fredericksburg.com/news/local/stafford-superintendent-apologizes-to-transgender-student-amid-national-outcry/article_8d0f967a-2092-57c0-9328-33a68a084c15.html Accessed August 7, 2019.

p. 16, "High testosterone is…" "Sports Gender Controversy—Bonus Scene," Gender Revolution: A Journey with Katie Couric, *National Geographic*, February 5, 2017, https://www.youtube.com/watch?v=qFFPcIcAUUs Accessed August 7, 2019.

p. 17, "I'm going to keep on doing…" "Diamond League: Caster Semenya Wins 800m in Doha Two Days After Losing Ruling Against IAAF," BBC, May 3, 2019, https://www.bbc.com/sport/athletics/48153742 Accessed August 7, 2019.

p. 28, "You're making people uncomfortable…" Janet Mock, as told to Kierna Mayo, "I Was Born A Boy,"

Marie Claire, May 18, 2011, https://www.marieclaire.com/sex-love/advice/a6075/born-male/ Accessed August 7, 2019.

p. 32, "We've moved beyond the idea that…" Billy Porter on *The Late Show with Stephen Colbert*, June 13, 2019, https://www.youtube.com/watch?v=fY058WwzR7s Accessed August 7, 2019.

p. 43, "Within most of these cultures …" Genny Beemyn, "Transgender History in the United States," in *Trans Bodies, Trans Selves*, ed. Laura Erickson-Schroth. New York: Oxford University Press, 2014, p. 6. https://www.umass.edu/stonewall/sites/default/files/Infoforandabout/transpeople/genny_beemyn_transgender_history_in_the_united_states.pdf Accessed August 7, 2019.

p. 47, "The news of the transgender military ban…" Petty Officer 2nd Class Megan Winters, "What It Meant to Attend the State of the Union, as a Transgender Service Member," Lamba Legal (blog), February 6, 2019, https://www.lambdalegal.org/blog/20190206_transgender-service-member-sotu Accessed August 7, 2019.

SELECT BIBLIOGRAPHY

Books

Gonzales, Maya. *The Gender Wheel*. San Francisco, CA: Reflection Press, 2017.

Iantaffi, Alex, and Meg-John Barker. *How to Understand Your Gender: A Practical Guide for Exploring Who You Are*. Philadelphia, PA: Jessica Kingsley Publishers, 2018.

Jimerson, Tristan, and Archie Bongiovanni. *A Quick & Easy Guide to They/Them Pronouns*. Portland, OR: Limerence Press, 2018.

Kidd, Kenneth B. *Making American Boys: Boyology and the Feral Tale*. Minneapolis, MN: University of Minnesota Press, 2004.

Stevenson, Robin. *Pride: Celebrating Diversity & Community*. Victoria, BC, Canada: Orca Book Publishers, 2016.

Websites, Articles, and Documentaries

Abbot, Karen, "The Mystery of Murray Hall," *Smithsonian Magazine*, July 27, 2011, https://www.smithsonianmag.com/history/the-mystery-of-murray-hall-35612997/ Accessed April 15, 2019.

Amnesty International, "No Safe Place," November 2017, https://www.unhcr.org/en-us/5a2ee5a14.pdf Accessed May 20, 2019.

Balingit, Moriah, "Education Department No Longer Investigating Transgender Bathroom Complaints," *The Washington Post*, February 12, 2018, https://www.washingtonpost.com/news/education/wp/2018/02/12/education-department-will-no-longer-investigate-transgender-bathroom-complaints/?utm_term=.626445a3aafa Accessed August 7, 2019.

Blum, Robert, M.D., et al., "It Begins at 10: How Gender Expectations Shape Early Adolescence Around the World." *Journal of Adolescent Health* 61, no. 4, Supplement, October 2017, pp. S3-S4, https://doi.org/10.1016/j.jadohealth.2017.07.009 Accessed August 7, 2019.

Chandra-Mouli, V., et al., "Implications of the Global Early Adolescent Study's Formative Research Findings for Action and for Research," *Journal of Adolescent Health* 61, no. 4, Supplement, October 2017, pp. S5-S9. https://doi.org/10.1016/j.jadohealth.2017.07.012 Accessed August 7, 2019

Couric, Katie. *Gender Revolution*, directed by Michael Del Monte. New York: National Geographic, 2017. TV documentary film.

Hains, Rebecca, "Can Gender Specific Toys Affect a Child's Development?" CBC Radio, 2017. https://www.cbc.ca/radio/thecurrent/the-current-for-december-18-2017-1.4451239/can-gender-specific-toys-affect-a-child-s-development-researchers-weigh-in-1.4451295 Accessed August 7, 2019.

Hesse, Monica, "We Celebrated Michael Phelps's Genetic Differences. Why Punish Caster Semenya for Hers?" *The Washington Post*, May 2, 2019, https://www.washingtonpost.com/lifestyle/style/we-celebrated-michael-phelpss-genetic-differences-why-punish-caster-semenya-for-hers/2019/05/02/93d08c8c-6c2b-11e9-be3a-33217240a539_story.html Accessed May 5, 2019.

Hughes, Catherine, and Rebecca Hughes, "Womenomics is Flipping the Script on Men in Japan," *Fortune*, March 6, 2019, http://fortune.com/2019/03/06/japan-economic-empowerment-gender-equality/ Accessed May 20, 2019.

Kralik, Joellen, and Jennifer Palmer, "Bathroom Bill Legislative Tracking," July 28, 2017, http://www.ncsl.org/research/education/-bathroom-bill-legislative-tracking635951130.aspx Accessed May 20, 2019.

Lahood, Grant. *Intersexion: Gender Ambiguity Unveiled*. Film. Ponsonby Productions Limited. 2012.

Let Toys Be Toys, "Who's in the Picture? Gender Stereotypes and Toy Catalogues," December 2017, http://lettoysbetoys.org.uk/wp-content/uploads/2012/12/LetToysBeToys-Catalogues-report-Dec17.pdf Accessed August 7, 2019.

Levy, Diane, et al., "A Paired-Testing Pilot Study of Housing Discrimination Against Same-Sex Couples and Transgender Individuals," Urban Institute, June 30, 2017, https://www.urban.org/research/publication/paired-testing-pilot-study-housing-discrimination-against-same-sex-couples-and-transgender-individuals Accessed June 3, 2019.

Love, Barbara, "Developing a Liberatory Consciousness," *Readings for Diversity and Social Justice*. eds. Maurianne Adams, et al., Carlton College, https://apps.carleton.edu/campus/intercultural/assets/dev_liberatory_conscious_001.pdf Accessed June 10, 2019.

Mock, Janet, as told to Kierna Mayo, "I Was Born a Boy," *Marie Claire*, May 18, 2011, https://www.marieclaire.com/sex-love/advice/a6075/born-male/ Accessed May 20, 2019.

Nordberg, Jenny, "I'm a Woman Who Lived as a Boy: My Years as a Bacha Posh," *Time*, September 15, 2014, http://time.com/3379066/afghan-woman-boy-bacha-posh/ Accessed May 20, 2019.

Russell, Stephen, "Chosen Name Use Is Linked to Reduced Depressive Symptoms, Suicidal Ideation, and Suicidal Behavior Among Transgender Youth," *Journal of Adolescent Medicine* 63, no. 4, October 2018, https://doi.org/10.1016/j.jadohealth.2018.02.003 Accessed June 8, 2019.

Strochlic, Nina, "Inside the Lives of Girls Dressed as Boys in Afghanistan," *National Geographic*, March 2, 2018, https://www.nationalgeographic.com/photography/proof/2018/march/bacha-posh-gender-afghanistan/ Accessed June 9, 2019.

Talbot, Margaret, "About a Boy," *New Yorker*, March 11, 2013, https://www.newyorker.com/magazine/2013/03/18/about-a-boy-2 Accessed May 15, 2019.

Toomey, Russell, et al., "Transgender Adolescent Suicide Behavior," *Pediatrics* 42, no. 4, October 2018. https://pediatrics.aappublications.org/content/142/4/e20174218?sso=1&sso_redirect_count=1&nfstatus=401&nftoken=00000000-0000-0000-0000-000000000000&nfstatusdescription=ERROR%3a+No+local+token Accessed June 7, 2019.

Vaughan, Alden T., "The Sad Case of Thomas(ine) Hall," *The Virginia Magazine of History and Biography* 86, no. 2, 1978, pp. 146–148, www.jstor.org/stable/4248200 Accessed April 7, 2019.

Watson, Julie, and Jennifer McDermott, "Transgender Care Cost Military Less than 1 Percent of its Health Budget Since 2010," PBS, February 27, 2019, https://www.pbs.org/newshour/nation/military-spent-about-8-million-on-transgender-care-since-2016 Accessed June 9, 2019.

About the Author

Rebecca Stanborough has two children, three cats, and a Master of Fine Arts in writing for children and young adults. Her books include *Sexual Harassment in the Age of #MeToo* in this series and others in the Daring Women series. She writes and teaches middle school English Language Arts in St. Augustine, Florida.

INDEX